What To Do When There's No One But You

by Harriet Margolis Gore

illustrated by David Lindroth

PRENTICE HALL, INC., ENGLEWOOD CLIFFS, N.J.

Printed in the United States of America · J

Prentice-Hall International, Inc., London
Prentice-Hall of Australia, Pty. Ltd., North Sydney
Prentice-Hall of Canada, Ltd., Toronto
Prentice-Hall of India Private Ltd., New Delhi
Prentice-Hall of Japan, Inc., Tokyo

Library of Congress Cataloging in Publication Data

Gore, Harriet.
    What to do when there's no one but you.

    SUMMARY: Stories illustrate common first aid
problems, from cuts to broken bones, and show step
-by-step illustrated instructions for caring for
these injuries.
    1. First aid in illness and injury—Juvenile
literature. [1. First aid] I. Lindroth, David,
illus. II. Title.
RC86.5.G67   614.8'8   73-13939
ISBN 0-13-955070-4

Table of Contents

introduction

No matter how careful people are, accidents do happen. What you do to care for someone who is hurt is called first aid. This book shows how kids can help themselves and others until adult help comes. Sometimes knowing first aid makes the difference between a good time and a bad time.

The most important thing to do when a serious accident takes place is to get help. If an adult is around, you can shout. If no adult is around, call the operator and tell her your name and location and what kind of help you think you need.

Most accidents are not that serious. The important thing is to stay calm and to keep the person who is hurt calm. Act deliberately rather than quickly, to help keep the injured person comfortable and safe from further injury.

Anthony's Peanut Butter Sandwich

Anthony loved peanut butter. He put it on everything—even on spaghetti and ice cream.

One day he was very hungry so he took out a loaf of bread, a jar of peanut butter, and a sharp knife.

"Hmm, what's this red stuff? I didn't put jelly on my bread," he said to himself. "Oh my, it's blood. I've cut myself with the knife."

Anthony took a clean napkin and pressed it firmly on his cut. He held it there for a few minutes until the bleeding stopped. He washed the cut with soap and water and covered it with a Band-aid.

He made a compress by wrapping an ice cube in a clean napkin. He held it to his finger until it stopped hurting.

Then Anthony fixed another peanut butter sandwich and ate it all up!

① He took a clean napkin and pressed it firmly on his cut.

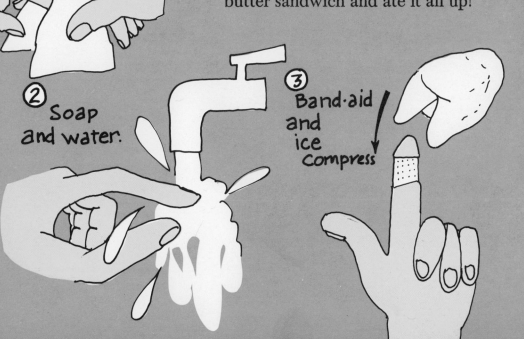

② Soap and water.

③ Band-aid and ice compress

The Day It Snowed Inside

Keith and Anthony were having a pillow fight. Rrrip. . . . The pillow had torn. The feathers were everywhere.

"Yippee! It's snowing," laughed Anthony.

But the feathers tickled Anthony's nose. He sneezed and sneezed. He sneezed so hard that his nose started to bleed.

"Sit down, lean over forward, and pinch your nostrils tightly. Then put this cold compress on it."

"Sit down, lean over forward, and pinch your nostrils tightly. I'll make a cold compress for you to hold on your nose while you're pinching it," said Keith.

Anthony had to pinch his nose for ten minutes before the bleeding stopped.

Keith and Anthony cleaned up the feathers so Anthony wouldn't have to blow his nose again.

The Apple That Grew a Tooth

"My apple just grew a tooth!"

Press tissue on gum until it stops bleeding.

"Holy cow, look at this. My apple just grew a tooth!" said Matthew.

"You are only kidding, Matthew. That's your tooth. When you bit into the apple, that loose tooth fell out."

Matthew smiled.

"See, your gum is bleeding," said Michelle. "Take this tissue and press it on your gum until the bleeding stops."

Sure enough, the bleeding did stop. That night Matthew put the tooth under his pillow. In the morning, he found a shiny dime in its place.

He found a shiny dime in its place.

Wendy, The Princess

One day Wendy dressed up in her mother's old evening gown and high heels. She looked very elegant. She pretended she was a princess walking down the grand staircase.

Then Wendy tripped and fell down. She scraped her knee and, boy, did it hurt! She washed the scrape with soap and water, gently dried it, and covered it with a Band-aid. She put an ice compress on it.

"Next time," she thought, "I'll pretend I'm Tarzan. No more wobbly high heels for me."

The Secret Hideout

Wendy and Matthew found a pile of wood in a vacant lot.

"Let's build a secret hideout," said Wendy.

"I'll go get my father's hammer and nails," cried Matthew.

Soon Matthew came back with a hammer and a jar of nails. He began to hammer and immediately stuck a nail into his finger.

"You'd better tell your mother about that finger," Wendy advised when Matthew stopped groaning.

"Oh, it's just a tiny hole and it's not even bleeding," he said. "Besides, I'm not supposed to use Dad's tools without asking. I'm not telling anyone."

"Are you crazy?" shouted Wendy. "Don't you know that a tetanus germ could get into your body through that tiny hole! You'd better tell your mother so she can check with your doctor to see if you need a tetanus booster—it will protect you."

"Oh, okay," Matthew said. "And even if I don't need a booster shot, I'll wash out my sore and cover it with a Band-aid so it won't get infected."

A New Use For Frozen Food

"Ouch," shouted Wendy as she closed the drawer on her fingers.

When Keith came into the kitchen, she told him what happened. "And, boy, did they hurt!" she said.

"Your fingers are getting puffy, Wendy. We can stop the swelling with ice," said Keith.

"Hey, we can use a package of frozen food instead," said Wendy. "I can use frozen peas for bumps on my head, frozen juice for bumps on my arm, and frozen carrots when I bump my knee."

"I think just plain ice works a lot better," Keith grinned. "Come on, let's ask your mother to make sure none of your fingers are broken."

The Hottest Day

It was 90 degrees outside, even at the beach where Michelle and Anthony were spending the day.

"Phew! I sure feel weak and dizzy. Maybe I have sunstroke," said Anthony.

"You've been in the sun too long," Michelle said. "Your skin feels cool and sweaty and that's a sign of heat exhaustion. Let's lie in the shade for a while. These potato chips and this grape juice will make you feel better."

In a little while Anthony did feel better.

"What would you have done if I really had sunstroke?"

"You would have had a temperature, and your skin would be *hot and dry*. I'd have cooled you down with water and taken you straight to a doctor. But all you have is a little sunburn," said Wendy, handing him the cold cream. "Here, spread some of this on. . . . and pass the potato chips."

The Coldest Day

One blistery winter morning, Anthony and Michelle were building a snowman in the 20-degree weather.

"Let's go inside. My hands are so cold and numb, I probably have frostbite!" cried Anthony.

"Don't worry, you're not frostbitten. If you were, your hands would turn blue and numb. Not red like yours," said Michelle.

Anthony made a face. "Well, they sure feel frozen. Maybe they'll warm up if I rub them together."

"You know what? If you did have frostbite, you wouldn't rub your hands like that. You'd let them warm up *slowly* by covering them or putting them in warm water. Or you could put them under your armpits like this and let your body heat warm them.

"Forget it," said Anthony. "I'm going inside now to get some hot soup to warm my poor stomach."

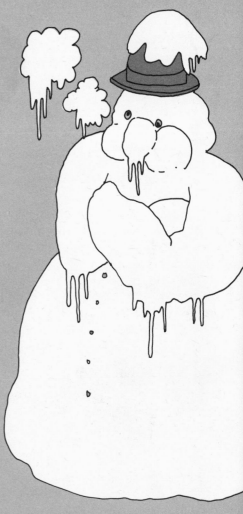

The Poison Ivy Picnic

Wendy and Anthony were on a picnic in the back yard. "Uh, oh," said Wendy. "I think this stuff we're sitting in is poison ivy!"

"We're surrounded," Anthony shouted. So they packed up their lunch, and went home. They took off their clothes to wash them, and washed very carefully with soap and water.

Anthony scratched a few poison ivy blisters on his wrist. "Don't do that," Wendy told him. "Use some of this calamine lotion to keep it from itching."

While Anthony put calamine lotion on his wrist, Wendy drew pictures of poisonous plants and taped them to the lid of their picnic basket.

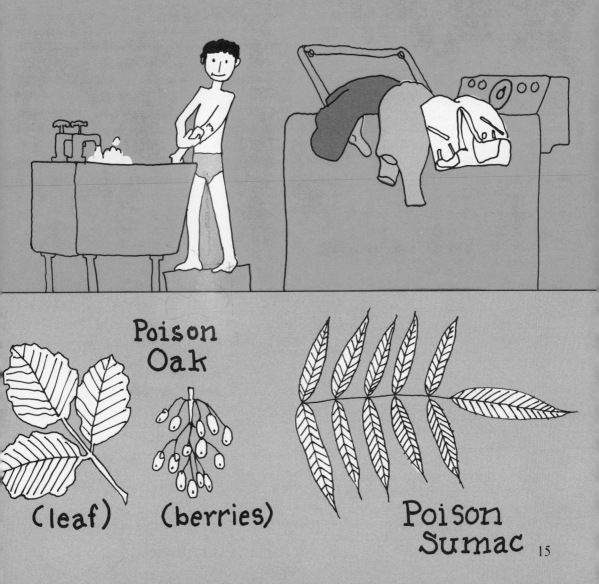

Poison
Oak

(leaf)   (berries)

Poison
Sumac

The Experiment That Backfired

SPLASH!

DON'T RUB EYE!!

One afternoon, while Keith was playing with his chemistry set, some acid splashed into his eye. It burned! He ran to the sink and put his eye under the faucet.

Keith washed his eye in tepid water for ten minutes until the chemical was out.

It was hard to keep his eye open.

"I know I'd better not rub my eye. I'll cover it with a sterile gauze pad and ask Mom to have it checked," thought Keith. "And next time I'll wear my safety glasses when I'm experimenting."

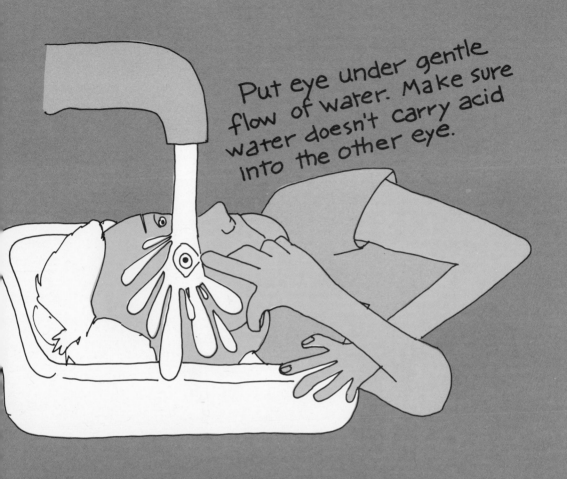

Put eye under gentle flow of water. Make sure water doesn't carry acid into the other eye.

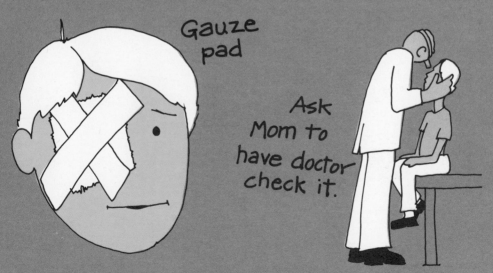

Gauze pad

Ask Mom to have doctor check it.

A Sad Story with a Happy Ending

"Help!! My sleeve is on fire!"

She dropped to the floor.

Wendy and Michelle were making hot chocolate in the kitchen.

"Help, my sleeve is on fire!" shouted Wendy.

She remembered that fire climbs upward so she dropped down to the floor. Michelle rolled the rug over Wendy's arm to smother the flames. Then she filled a pot with cool water and poured the water over Wendy's arm.

The fire was out!

Wendy's arm was burned and blistered. A piece of sleeve stuck to her burned arm. Michelle knew she must not remove it. She covered the burn with plastic wrap. She poured Wendy a glass of water and then called the doctor.

Then she slipped a pillow under Wendy's arm.

"I'll put an ice compress on it to help the pain," Michelle told her.

"I'll roll my sleeves up the next time I use the stove," Wendy said on the way to the doctor.

"Now we know why your mother doesn't let us cook when she's not home," added Michelle.

A blanket smothers the flame

Cool water

She covered the burn with plastic wrap. Burnt arm should be raised.

19

Wendy Gets Bugged

"Yipes! A bug just flew into my ear. I can hear it buzzing," said Wendy.

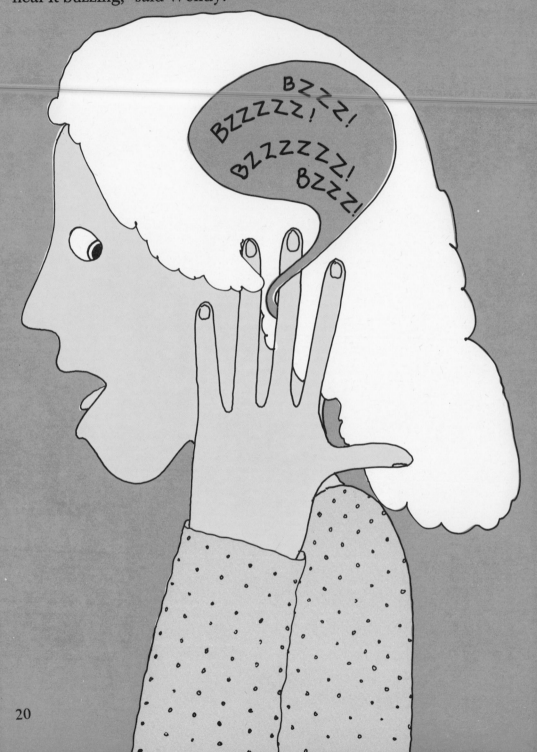

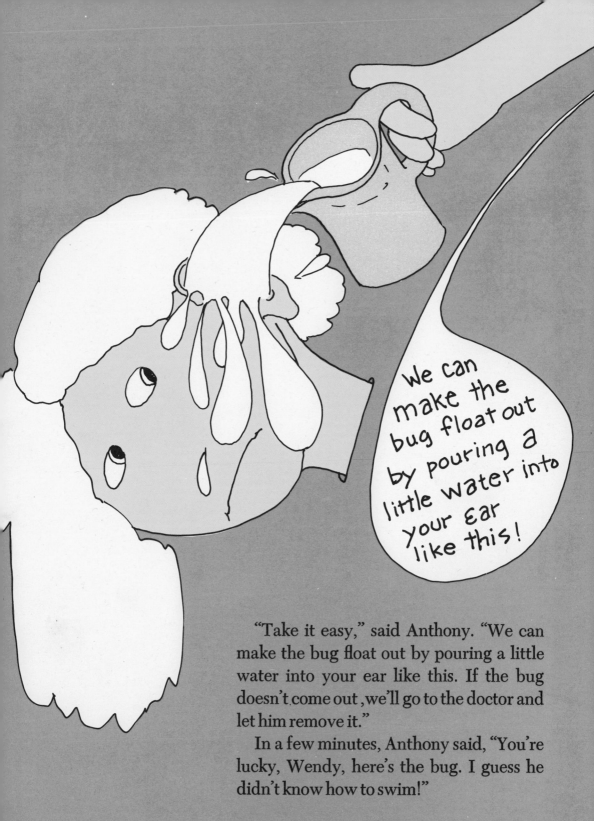

"Take it easy," said Anthony. "We can make the bug float out by pouring a little water into your ear like this. If the bug doesn't come out, we'll go to the doctor and let him remove it."

In a few minutes, Anthony said, "You're lucky, Wendy, here's the bug. I guess he didn't know how to swim!"

Keith's Big Fish

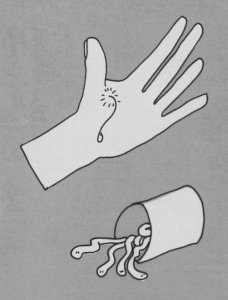

Keith and his Uncle Ed went on a fishing trip. Keith had already caught one big fish and now he was baiting his line.

"Ouch, I've stuck myself with the fish hook."

"Hey, don't rock the boat, Keith. It only went in a little way. I'll pull it out for you."

Uncle Ed cleaned out the wound with peroxide and put a clean bandage on it.

"I know I've had a tetanus booster this year so I'm protected," said Keith.

"You know," said Uncle Ed, "if that hook had gone in farther, we would have had to push it through and cut off the barb. I always have a doctor do that. If it's done right, your finger doesn't become infected.

Keith smiled in relief.

"Thanks a lot for fixing me up, Uncle Ed. Now I just have one question."

"What's that, Keith?"

"Why don't we start our campfire and fry some of those fish for supper?"

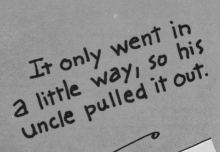

It only went in a little way, so his uncle pulled it out.

If the hook had gone in farther, the doctor would have had to push it through and cut the barb off.

To Bee Or Not To Bee

"What a huge daisy patch. I think I'll surprise Mom with some flowers," thought Anthony. But he didn't notice the bee sitting on one of the daisies when he picked it.

Ice Compress

"Yikes! I've been stung!" he cried out.

He ran back to the house and put an ice compress to his hand. When it stopped hurting, he asked his mother to remove the little stinger with tweezers.

"Always let somebody know when you've been stung," she told him, "because some people are allergic to bee stings and need to see the doctor right away."

Use tweezers, but don't squeeze poison sac.

sac

Michelle's New Puppy

Michelle's new puppy wanted the ball she was holding. He jumped up and grabbed it from her.

"Ouch," she cried as the puppy bit her hand. "I'd better wash the bite with soap and water right away," she thought.

After she washed it, she pressed a gauze pad on it until the bleeding stopped. Then she covered it with a Band-aid and put an ice compress on it.

"I'll ask Mom if I need a tetanus booster. I'm glad it was *my* puppy. I know he's had a rabies shot. If a strange dog had bitten me, it would have to be caught and watched for rabies."

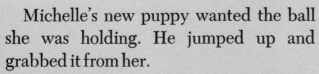

gauze pad

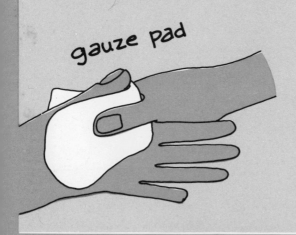

① Wash bite with soap & water.

② Press with gauze pad until bleeding stops.

③ Band-aid & ice compress.

A Snake Story

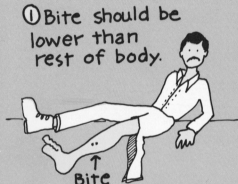

① Bite should be lower than rest of body.

Bite

② Tie belt around leg.

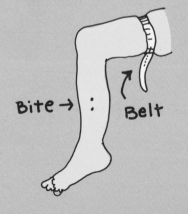

Bite → | : | ← Belt

"I love camping," said Keith.

"So do I," added his Uncle Ed. "Say, did I ever tell you the story about my rattlesnake bite?"

"Were you poisoned?"

"I could have died," said Uncle Ed, "but my friend made me lie still with the leg with the bite lower than the rest of me. He tied his belt around my leg above the bite. Then he let the bite bleed a little and loosened the belt for a minute every fifteen minutes. He sterilized the blade of his pocket knife with a match to kill the germs on it and cut a small, shallow cross over the bite."

"What was that for?" asked Keith.

"Well, after he made the cut, he sucked on the bite for about an hour."

"Didn't your friend get poisoned too?"

"No, because he was careful not to swallow any poison."

"Then what happened?" Keith wanted to know.

"Afterwards, he put a cold, wet cloth on the bite. He kept very calm and told me to stay still to keep the poison from going through my body. I'll never forget my friend. And ever since then, I take a snake bite kit with me whenever I camp."

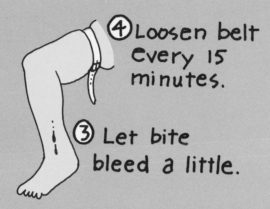

④ Loosen belt every 15 minutes.

③ Let bite bleed a little.

⑤ Sterilize the blade with a match.

⑥ Cut a shallow cross above the bite.

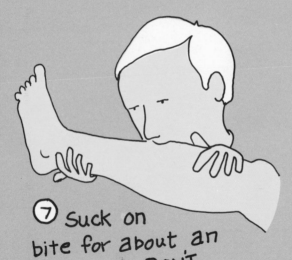

⑦ Suck on bite for about an hour, but DON'T SWALLOW ANY POISON.

⑧ Put a cold, wet cloth on the bite.

Matthew's Eye

One windy day, Matthew was playing outside and a cinder blew in his eye. His eye began to water. Boy, did he want to rub it, but instead he covered it with his hand and did not rub it.

He covered it with his hand and DID NOT RUB IT.

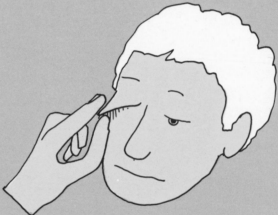

He pulled the top lid of his eye over the bottom. Some of the dirt came out. He went home and washed his eye with water. Later on, he went to the doctor to have his eye checked even though it felt better.

"The cinder scratched your eye slightly," the doctor told Keith. "Use this medicine and it will heal. It's always a good idea to have your eye checked when something gets in it or hits you. If you ever get hit in the eye with something hard like a ball, put a cold compress on it. And then have it checked by a doctor."

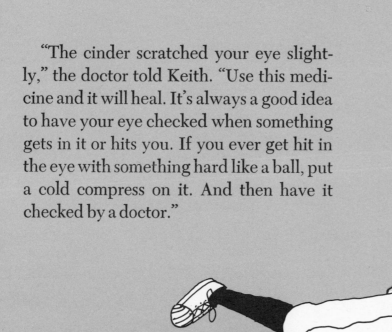

"If you ever get hit in the eye with something hard, put a cold compress on it. Then have it checked by a doctor."

Michelle's Old Broom

"Ouch, I just got a splinter," cried Michelle, as she was sweeping the porch.

She went into the house and got the tweezer. She grabbed the splinter and gently pulled it out the same way it went in. She then washed her hand with soap and water and covered the puncture with a Band-aid. She called her doctor to see if she needed a tetanus booster.

tweezer

The next day, while sweeping, she got another splinter!

"That settles it. We need to buy a new broom," she thought.

This time the splinter went in deep. She asked her mother to take it out.

"Wow, this splinter is nearly an inch long!" she said.

"Yes, and I had better throw it away before I sit on it by mistake!" her mother laughed.

31

Don't Talk With Your Mouth Full!

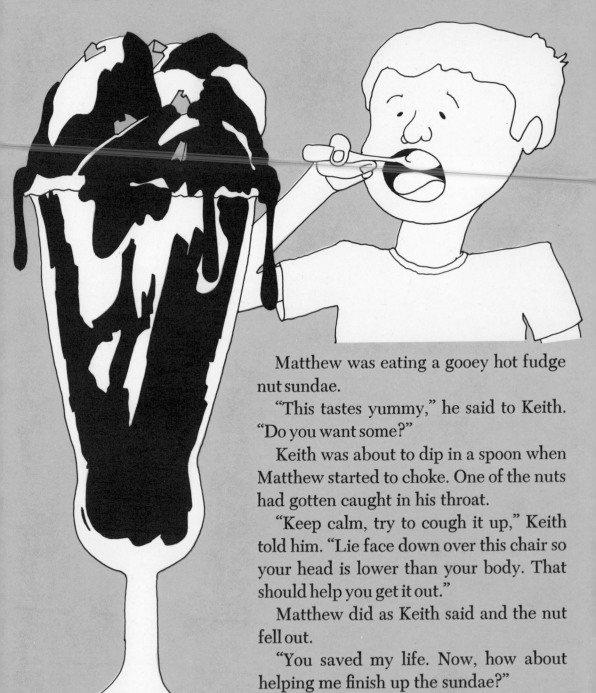

Matthew was eating a gooey hot fudge nut sundae.

"This tastes yummy," he said to Keith. "Do you want some?"

Keith was about to dip in a spoon when Matthew started to choke. One of the nuts had gotten caught in his throat.

"Keep calm, try to cough it up," Keith told him. "Lie face down over this chair so your head is lower than your body. That should help you get it out."

Matthew did as Keith said and the nut fell out.

"You saved my life. Now, how about helping me finish up the sundae?"

"Sure," Keith grinned, "but you can keep the nuts."

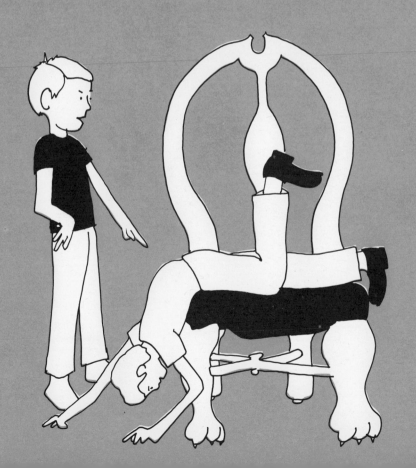

A Shocking Story

"What's wrong with this toaster?" Michelle grumbled.

"It's burning up my toast!" She stuck her knife into the toaster to pull it out. "Stop!" Anthony shouted. "Unplug it first."

It was too late. Michelle got a shock.

Anthony grabbed the broom and knocked Michelle away from the toaster with its wooden handle.

"Now do you see why you shouldn't put a knife in the toaster?" he asked.

"I'd always wondered," Michelle admitted as she buttered her toast.

He knocked
her away from the
toaster with a wooden
broom handle.

Anthony wanted to grow up big and strong. He knew that vitamins help you grow. One day, Anthony made a terrible mistake. He thought that if he ate a lot of vitamins, he'd grow up even stronger.

When Michelle found the empty bottle, she gave him 3 glasses of milk to drink. Then she called the Poison Control Center. She told them the kind of vitamins Anthony had swallowed and they told her what to do.

"You could have poisoned yourself, dummy. Just because a little bit is good for you doesn't mean that you should take more," Michelle said.

"I'll never make that mistake again," said Anthony.

Anthony wanted to grow up big and strong.

When Michelle found the empty bottle, she gave him 3 glasses of milk. Then she called the Poison Control Center.

Poisoning

1. Act quickly. GIVE WATER OR MILK TO DRINK FOR ALL POISONS. This slows down the poison.
2. Call the Poison Control Center or dial "Operator" for help.
3. Try to find out what the poison is by checking the container. Save the bottle or container the poison was in. If you don't know what has been taken and the person vomits, save the vomit so it can be checked.
4. Some poisons can be vomited. You can make the person vomit by tickling the back of his throat with your finger. Make sure his head is lower than his body. (If an adult is around, he can give syrup of ipecac to make the person vomit. This can be bought at a drugstore and should only be used in an emergency. The person must have lots of liquid in his stomach for it to work.) Do not try to make a person who is not awake vomit.
5. Some poisons can burn the mouth and stomach or get into the lungs. DON'T MAKE THE PERSON VOMIT if these are swallowed.

Poisons That Can Be Vomited

Aftershave lotion
Aspirin
Bubble bath
Cough medicine
Deodorant
Nail polish
Nail polish remover
Perfume
Plants
Poisonous berries
Poisonous mushrooms
Rubbing alcohol
Shampoo
Skin lotion
Vitamins

Poisons That Must Not Be Vomited

Bleach
Cleaning fluid
Dishwasher detergent
Drain cleaner
Furniture polish
Gasoline
Household ammonia

Insect poison
Kerosene
Liquid paint
Lye
Toilet bowl cleaner
Turpentine

Painting the House

Matthew and his father were painting their house. His father was on the ladder. Crash! He fell off.

"Help me up," said his father.

Help me up!

Oh no! You'd better stay flat and don't move. Your back and neck may be hurt.

"Oh no, you'd better stay flat and don't move. Your back and neck may be hurt. You have to be moved carefully so your neck and back stay straight. I'll cover you with a blanket and put a cold compress on that bump on your head."

Matthew went into the house. He picked up the telephone and dialed "0." He told the operator what had happened and gave her his name and address. She sent an ambulance.

Blanket and cold compress.

He dialed "O." He told the operator what had happened and gave her his NAME and ADDRESS.

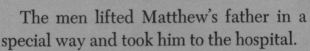

The men lifted Matthew's father in a special way and took him to the hospital.

"Your father was not badly hurt because you made sure he stayed still until we could move him properly," said the doctor.

"I'm glad I did the right thing," said Matthew.

His father smiled because he was glad too.

Help, I Have Hiccoughs!

"Boo!" said Anthony to Michelle. He was making the scariest face he could.

"What on earth are you two doing?" asked Wendy. "This isn't Halloween."

"Michelle has the hiccoughs and I'm trying to scare her so they'll go away."

"But it's not (hic) working (hic)," cried Michelle.

"Try this. Hold your breath for about a minute," said Anthony.

"That doesn't (hic) work either (hic)," Michelle moaned.

"You can always drink a glass of water slowly," Wendy suggested.

Michelle sipped a glass of water.

"It worked, my hiccoughs are gone," said Michelle, smiling.

"My way was much more fun though," muttered Anthony.

Keith's Figure Eight

Keith and Wendy went skating on the lake.

"Watch me, Wendy, I'm going to do a figure eight," Keith shouted.

Splat! He slipped on the ice and fell. He landed on his hand.

"Help, Wendy, I think I've broken my wrist," cried Keith.

"Take your good hand and slide it under your other hand and hold it straight like this. Put this ice on it. Broken bones have to be kept as straight as possible. Don't let it flop around," said Wendy.

"Keith went to the doctor. The doctor took an X-ray picture of the bone. He put a cast on Keith's wrist. Wendy was the first to sign it.

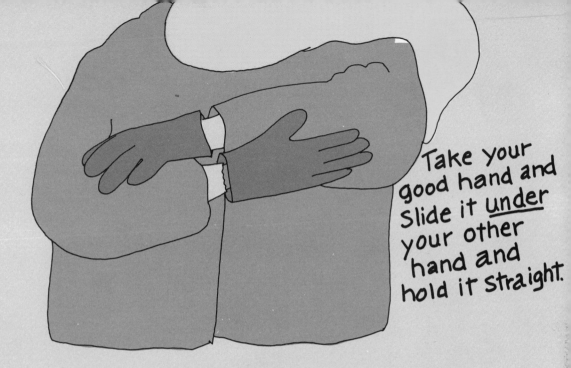

Take your good hand and slide it <u>under</u> your other hand and hold it straight.

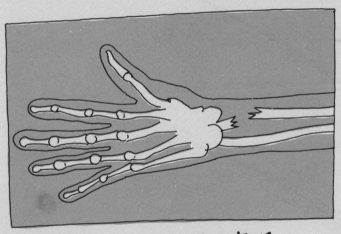

An X-RAY of Keith's wrist.

The doctor put a cast on Keith's wrist.

The Winners

Keith, Wendy, Michelle, and Anthony were taking turns pretending to be contestants on a T.V. quiz show.

"Congratulations, Keith and Michelle. You have just won a car, a boat, and $1,000," announced Matthew, the master of ceremonies.

"Oh, I'm so excited, I think I'm going to faint!" exclaimed Michelle.

"Quick, put her down flat on the floor and raise her legs on this folded coat. Loosen her collar and rub her arms," said Wendy.

"Maybe I shouldn't give her all those presents at once if she gets so excited that she faints," laughed Matthew.

"I'm okay, I'm okay," said Michelle. "Give me my prizes!"

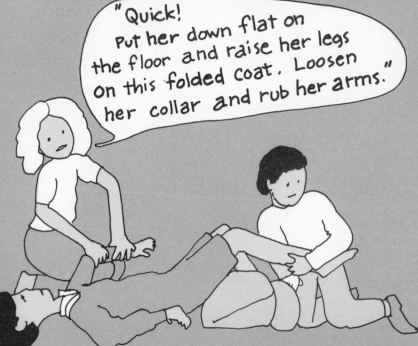

Wendy Learns About Resuscitation

One night Matthew and Wendy were watching T.V. "Look at how that kid saved the man's life, just by breathing!" Matthew said.

"I wonder how they do that," Wendy murmured.

"It's called mouth-to-mouth resuscitation. If you're willing to work at it, I'll show you how," said their father. "We learned to do that for the Rescue League. But you have to promise that you will never do it unless you are sure that the person is not breathing."

"How can you tell?" Wendy asked.

"You can check that by putting your ear next to the person's nose or mouth. If he is breathing, you will feel warm air and hear a rhythmic sound. Then check his chest to see if it is moving up and down. If you are absolutely sure he's not breathing, here's what you do:

1. Turn his head to the side and clean out the mouth with your finger.
2. Lift his neck. Pull his chin upward.
3. Check breathing.
4. Pinch the nostrils shut. Take a deep breath. Place your mouth over his and blow. Remove your mouth to let the air out. Listen for air coming out. Watch the chest fall. Repeat. Blow once every five seconds for an adult and once every three seconds for a child.

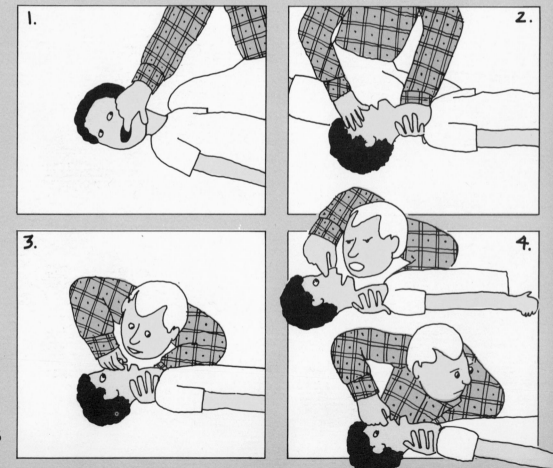

"You can also restore someone's breathing with mouth-to-nose resuscitation:
1. Turn his head to the side and clean out the nose gently with your fingers.
2. Lift his neck. Pull his chin upward.
3. Check breathing again.
4. Pinch the mouth shut. Take a deep breath. Place your mouth over his nose and blow into his nostrils. Remove your mouth and let the air out. Listen for air coming out of the victim's body. Watch his chest fall. Repeat. Blow once every five seconds for an adult and every three seconds for a child.

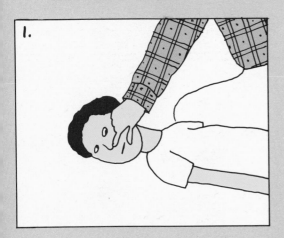

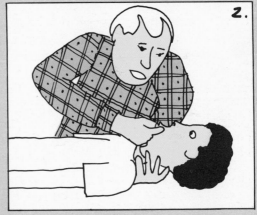

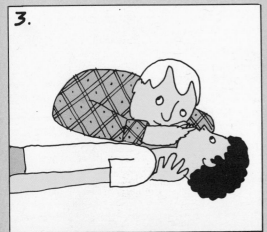

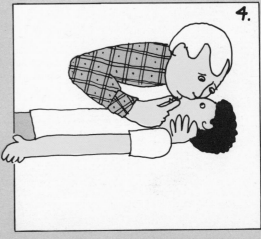

Index